5/06

The Beslan School Siege
and Separatist Terrorism

MICHAEL V. USCHAN

CURRICULUM CONSULTANT: MICHAEL M. YELL
National Board Certified Social Studies Teacher,
Hudson Middle School, Hudson, Wisconsin

WORLD ALMANAC® LIBRARY

Please visit our web site at: www.worldalmanaclibrary.com
For a free color catalog describing World Almanac® Library's list of high-quality books and multimedia programs, call 1-800-848-2928 (USA) or 1-800-387-3178 (Canada). World Almanac® Library's fax: (414) 332-3567.

Library of Congress Cataloging-in-Publication Data

Uschan, Michael V., 1948-
    The Beslan school siege and separatist terrorism / Michael V. Uschan.
        p. cm. – (Terrorism in today's world)
    Includes bibliographical references and index.
    ISBN 0-8368-6556-1 (lib. bdg.)
    ISBN 0-8368-6563-4 (softcover)
    1. Terrorism–Russia (Federation)–Beslan–Juvenile literature I. Title. II. Series
    HV6433.R9U83   2006
    947.5'2–dc22   2005043688

This North American edition first published in 2006 by
World Almanac® Library
A Member of the WRC Media Family of Companies
330 West Olive Street, Suite 100
Milwaukee, WI 53212 USA

Original edition copyright © 2004 The Brown Reference Group plc. This U.S. edition copyright © 2006 by World Almanac® Library.

Managing Editor: Tim Cooke
Designer: Steve Wilson
Picture Researcher: Laila Torsun
World Almanac® Library editor: Alan Wachtel
World Almanac® Library art direction: Tammy West
World Almanac® Library design: Dave Kowalski
World Almanac® Library production: Jessica Morris and Robert Kraus

Picture credits: Front Cover: Empics: NTV/AP BRG: 06; Corbis: Christian, Maury/ Sygma 40; Dal, S/Reuters 10; Jarekji, Ali/Reuters 36/37; Korotayev, Viktor/ Reuters 38; MCerlane, Paul/Reuters 41; Norov, Dmitry/Reuters 17; Reuters 15; Empics: AP/NTV 09; Sadulayveu, Musa/AP 23; Rex: Beliakov, Dmitry 04/05, Itar-Tass 21; Knolt, Herbert 28; Sipa Press 31, 32. Robert Hunt Library: 26; Topham: 24/25; Kulbis, M. 18; Novosti 12/13.

Printed in the United States of America

1 2 3 4 5 6 7 8 9 10 09 08 07 06

CONTENTS

Chapter 1 Beslan School Siege   4

Chapter 2 Chechen Separatists   12

Chapter 3 Separatist Terrorists   24

Chapter 4 Responses to Separatist Terrorism   36

Time Line   44

Glossary   45

Further Reading   46

Index   47

Cover photo: This image comes from a video the hostage takers made of themselves and their captives inside the school at Beslan early in the three-day siege in September 2004.

CHAPTER ONE

Beslan School Siege

The aim of terrorism is to spread terror. Terrorists seek to achieve their goals by using violence to make large numbers of people afraid enough to give in to their demands. Terrorist groups are usually small, and their actions, such as bombings and kidnappings, often have relatively few victims. Such acts, however, are planned to make whole societies or groups of people afraid of falling victim to similar attacks. Terrorists' aims vary: some believe that they are acting from religious motives, while others use violence to start a revolution that will overthrow a government. Separatist terrorists want independence for their region and the ability to govern themselves. This group includes the terrorists who took more than one thousand adults and children hostage in a school in the Russian town of Beslan in 2004.

Terrorists Seize the School

In the 21 republics of the Russian Federation, September 1 is the "Day of Knowledge." At schools across the nation, students and their families celebrate the start of the academic year. In 2004, in Beslan, a city of 34,000 people in the Russian Republic of North Ossetia, more than one thousand students, teachers, and parents gathered on a playground outside School Number One, which teaches students between seven and eighteen years of age.

At 9:30 A.M., the occasion was shattered when 32 terrorists roared up to the school in two vehicles. Wearing black ski masks and armed with guns and belts loaded with explosives, the invaders killed five policemen in a brief but fierce battle. One attacker

▼ Special troops of the Russian Spetsnaz Unit prepare to storm School Number One in Beslan, North Ossetia, on September 3, 2004. Separatist terrorists from Chechnya had held more than a thousand hostages inside the school for three days.

also died in the exchange of gunfire. In the confusion of the deadly assault, about 150 people fled for their lives.

The attackers then herded everyone else into the school, beginning their barbaric act of terrorism. Before the siege ended three days later in a chaotic mix of explosions and gunfire, 331 people—including 186 children—died and more than 700 were injured.

Who Were The Terrorists?

The terrorists who took over the school were members of Riyad al-Salikhin, an Islamic group whose name translates as "Gardens of the Righteous." They were separatists from the nearby republic of Chechnya. Like North Ossetia, Chechnya is one of the smaller republics of the Russian Federation, a vast nation that includes Russia and covers much of northern Asia. In terms of population, wealth, and political power, Russia dominates the federation, and it contains the nation's capital, Moscow.

For more than a decade, Chechen rebels had been fighting the Russians for control of their republic. Most of the rebels were Muslims. Muslim Chechens make up about 80 percent of Chechnya's 1.2 million people. Many want independence from Russia, which has dominated the Chechens' homeland for centuries—including the period from 1924 to 1991. During that time, Chechnya was part of the Soviet Union, a communist nation that included Russia and other republics. After the Soviet Union broke up in December 1991, Chechnya became part of the new Russian Federation. In

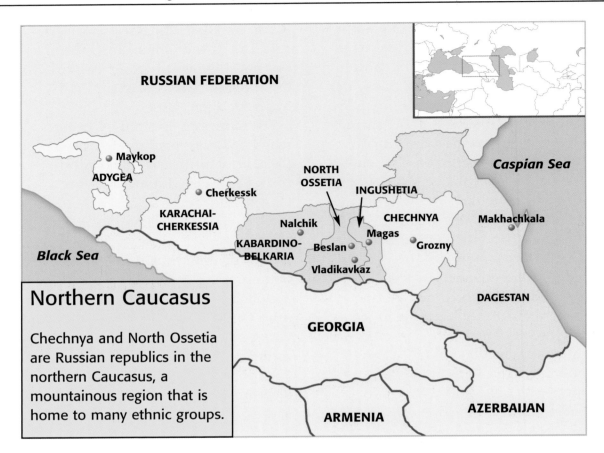

RUSSIAN FEDERATION

Maykop

ADYGEA

NORTH OSSETIA

INGUSHETIA

Caspian Sea

Cherkessk

KARACHAI-CHERKESSIA

Nalchik

CHECHNYA

Makhachkala

KABARDINO-BELKARIA

Magas

Beslan

Grozny

Black Sea

Vladikavkaz

DAGESTAN

Northern Caucasus

Chechnya and North Ossetia are Russian republics in the northern Caucasus, a mountainous region that is home to many ethnic groups.

GEORGIA

ARMENIA

AZERBAIJAN

the 1990s, Chechen rebels twice fought Russian forces but failed to win Chechnya's independence.

Some Chechens want Chechnya to remain part of the Russian Federation. Others support the creation of a separate state, but they believe that independence should be achieved by political means, not terrorism. But many rebels and other Chechens have adopted terrorist tactics to gain Chechnya's freedom. They think Russia's current military occupation of Chechnya is a continuation of the conflicts in the 1990s.

After seizing the school, the terrorists issued this statement: "We demand that the war in Chechnya be stopped immediately and that the withdrawal of [Russian] forces [from Chechnya] be carried out." They also made other demands, including the release of terrorists in neighboring Ingushetia and the resignation of Russian Federation president Vladimir Putin. Putin has refused to allow Chechnya to leave the Russian Federation and has maintained Russia's military occupation of the republic.

A Death Trap

The terrorists threatened to blow up the hostages if their demands were not met. When Putin rejected their

Why Beslan? Why Children?

As news of the Beslan school siege spread around the world, millions of people wondered why Chechen terrorists chose to attack a school in such a small, peaceful community. Beslan is in North Ossetia, whose residents are Christians and have always supported Russian control of the area. Russian president Vladimir Putin claims that the Muslim terrorists attacked Beslan in an attempt to involve other Muslims in the region in their ongoing conflict with Russia.

Many people have also wondered how the terrorists could have been so cruel as to target children in the attack. Margarita Komoyeva, a teacher who survived the siege, said a terrorist explained to her why he felt no remorse about the death of Beslan children: "One of them told me: 'Russian soldiers are killing our children in Chechnya, so we are here to kill yours.'"

The terrorists claimed on a Web site that "42,000 Chechen children of school age (have) been killed by Russian invaders." The site said that the children were among more than 250,000 Chechens who have died as a result of the long war over Chechnya. Human rights groups suggest the total number of civilian deaths in Chechnya is nearer to 50,000.

demands, a standoff developed. The terrorists moved their more than 1,100 hostages into the school's gymnasium, which was not much larger than a basketball court. Most of the hostages were students aged seven to eighteen but others ranged in age from infants to the elderly. The terrorists forced everyone to sit on the floor of the gym and then surrounded them with deadly explosive devices. They taped bombs to walls, suspended them from ceilings, and even put them in basketball hoops. Said one hostage: "They hung up explosives in the gym like Christmas baubles." The terrorists also planted bombs in other parts of the school.

The armed gunmen could easily detonate the explosives by pulling or putting pressure on a triggering device. The threat of this happening terrified the hostages into not trying to escape, and also helped protect the terrorists from being attacked by security forces.

Within hours after the siege began, hundreds of policemen, Russian soldiers, and members of elite anti-terrorist units ringed the school. Although the security forces outnumbered the terrorists and were better armed, they were afraid to attack because they feared the terrorists would kill the hostages. The terrorists had threatened to kill fifty hostages for every terrorist who was killed and twenty hostages for every terrorist injured. They put children in windows so snipers could not shoot them.

Eyewitness Accounts

Zarubek Tsumartov, a teenager, saw the terrorists seize the school but got away: "I was standing near the [school] gates, music was playing, when I saw three armed people running with guns. At first I thought it was a joke when they fired in the air [but then] we fled."

Marat Khamayev, age fifteen, on the treatment of hostages: "Initially we were escorted to the toilet together, then they stopped doing that and only took the little kids. The whole time they never let anybody sleep—if somebody dozed off they would shake him awake again, saying 'no sleeping!'"

Diana Gadzhinova, age fourteen, described the carnage from bombs that detonated in the gym: "I looked up and saw some children lying on the floor covered in blood and not moving. There was a dead lady lying beside me. Torn-off arms and legs were lying everywhere."

Oleg Tideyev, whose son survived, watched the end of the siege unfold from outside the school. He described how one terrorist died in the final battle: "I saw a wounded gunman fall out of the [school] window during the fighting. Militiamen were evacuating children nearby. When they saw the gunman, they tore him to bits within seconds. It felt like a venomous snake was being trampled."

The Hostages Suffer

For the hostages, their captivity was a terrible ordeal. One torment was the anguish of knowing they could die at any moment. Alla Gadieyeva, who survived along with her seven-year-old son and her mother said, "We were in complete fear, people were praying all the time." Ten-year-old Georgy Farniyev said the terrorists were ready to kill them for any reason: "They said: 'Sit down and if you make any noise, we will kill twenty children.'"

The hostages also suffered physically. The crowded gym became unbearably warm, and even taking off shirts and other clothing gave people little relief from the oppressive heat. The gym also became fouled with human waste because the terrorists refused to let people use the school's toilets.

Everyone became thirsty and hungry because the terrorists did not allow them food or water. They became so thirsty that some hostages drank their own urine. Fourteen-year-old Malik Kalchakeyev said that on the second day, women told boys to urinate into plastic bottles so children could drink the liquid to stay alive. "Small children, even babies drank it," he said. Fatima Kochieva, who was held hostage with her two children, said when they drank urine, a terrorist mocked them by saying, "Are you swines, are you?" But when she pleaded for water, he refused.

Adults kept many children from panicking. But Elena Kasumova, the school's deputy director, said her nine-year-old son Timur helped her remain calm. Timur massaged her feet, kissed her, and told her that when they were freed they could drink all the water they wanted. "He was so good to me," she said.

The Negotiations

Putin allowed Russian officials to negotiate with the terrorists via cell phones in an attempt to get the hostages released. At the same time, however, he refused to meet any of the terrorists' demands. The terrorists first talked with Leonid Roshal, a pediatrician they requested, who had been involved in negotiations with Chechen terrorists in a previous hostage situation. After the terrorists inside the school refused Roshal's plea to allow the hostages food and water, he claimed they were "very cruel people . . . a ruthless enemy."

On the second day of the siege, terrorists negotiated with Ruslan Aushev, the former president of the neighboring republic of Ingushetia. Aushev persuaded the terrorists to release twenty-six women who had babies with them. One mother, however, allowed her baby to go free but chose to stay with her other children.

The talks remained at a standstill on the third day (Friday, September 3), because Putin rejected all of the terrorists' demands. The terrorists agreed to allow unarmed men to remove dead bodies from the school. Shortly after these men arrived, at

▼ This picture, which is taken from a video made by the terrorists early in the siege, shows hostages crowded into the school gymnasium and explosives hung on wires from a basketball hoop.

1:05 P.M., two explosions rocked the school. The blasts signaled the beginning of the siege's final phase.

Death and Destruction

Although it is believed the explosions were accidental, no one is sure what happened. The eyewitness accounts do not agree. Some survivors from the siege claim that bombs taped to walls or basketball hoops fell to the ground, while others believe a hostage may have accidentally triggered one. Another report was that a bomb went off accidentally while a terrorist was checking it or moving it. Whatever the cause, the bombs devastated the gym. Fourteen-year-old Diana Gadzhinova remembered the initial blast: "There was [an] explosion above us and part of the ceiling fell in. People were screaming, there was panic."

The blasts killed and wounded many hostages and tore holes in the gym walls. When hostages began escaping through the openings, the terrorists shot them. "I saw one child go down and then another," said Kasumova. The explosions and gunfire startled police and soldiers surrounding the school. They stormed into the school to save as many lives as possible. Joining them were armed local residents seeking revenge on the captors of their sons, daughters, and wives. When the storming of the school began, the terrorists sent a telephone message to the security forces saying, "Best regards to Putin. Allahu Akbar (God is great)"—and started fighting back.

▼ Volunteers carry a wounded hostage to safety after the security forces stormed the school.

Beslan—One Year Later

Two new schools have been built to replace School Number One, which remains a shattered hulk. The destruction visible to everyone is symbolic of the psychological damage done to the hostages. Despite efforts by psychologists and social workers, many people from Beslan were still depressed and fearful a year after the attack.

Four-year-old Makharik Tskayev is one of the youngest survivors. His grandmother, Svet-lana Tskayeva, said he was frightened when she signed him up this year for kindergarten. The boy told her he feared "the men in the masks." Tskayeva also said his father has been unable tell Makharik that his mother and sister were killed. "We say simply that they are still in the school," she said. Roman Bichegov-Begoshvili claims he will never recover from the death of his nine-year-old son, Kazbek. "This sorrow," he said, "is enough for 110 years."

In the fierce battle that ensued, the terrorists detonated more bombs and security forces used powerful weapons including tanks, rocket launchers, and helicopter gunships. Hostages fled for their lives. Scores of hostages were killed in the crossfire between the terrorists and the security forces. Other hostages died in fires ignited by the fighting or were killed by debris falling from the damaged building.

Most of the hostages who died in the siege were killed during the fighting, which continued for several hours. Some of the terrorists escaped from the gymnasium and took refuge in other parts of the school or in nearby homes, where they were killed in shoot-outs with security forces. One terrorist was captured alive, when Russian troops saved him from local people who wanted to kill him. It is not known whether any of the terrorists managed to escape.

When the fighting ended, the school was littered with piles of dead bodies, including twelve dead soldiers. Many of the hundreds of injured hostages died in the following weeks and months. Marina Dzhukayeva-Tagziyeva died eleven months later, primarily from a head injury that initially left her in a coma for six months. Her two daughters both survived. At Marina's funeral her mother, Dusya Tagziyeva, said: "I ask God to punish the terrorists and their families! Let God never forgive the things they have done!"

The only terrorist known to survive, a Chechen carpenter named Nur-Pashi Kulayev, went on trial in 2005 on charges of murder and terrorism. Kulayev denied the charges. He said he had not known what the target of the operation was. If found guilty, Kulayev faces the death penalty, although the Russian Federation does not currently carry out executions.

CHAPTER TWO

Chechen Separatists

One day after the bloody end of the Beslan school siege, Russian Federation president Vladimir Putin claimed the attack had been staged with the help of Muslim terrorist groups from other countries. On September 4, 2004, Putin declared, "We are dealing with a direct intervention of international terror against Russia." He said that the terrorists included nine people from Arab countries and one from Africa.

Putin was never able to prove those claims. The terrorists whose bodies were identified after the end of the siege were Chechens and Ingush, Muslims from the neighboring republic of Ingushetia. Security analysts have long known that Muslims from other parts of the world do go to Chechnya to fight with the Chechens. Many Western observers and some Russian commentators, however, believed Putin was trying to link the school siege to the wider global struggle against terrorism that began after the September 11, 2001, terrorist attacks on the United States. They thought that Putin sought to gain more international support for his campaign against the Chechen separatists. In the past, many countries have criticized Russia's policies toward Chechnya as being repressive.

A Long, Troubled History

Chechnya lies in the Caucasus, a remote, rugged region bordering the Caucasus Mountains between the Black Sea and Caspian Sea. The Caucasus is home to more than thirty different ethnic groups, including the Chechens, who adopted Islam in the 1500s, after the region became part of the Turkish

▼ Grozny, the capital of Chechnya, was badly damaged during the 1990s in two wars fought between Chechen separatists and Russian military forces.

Ottoman Empire. Like their neighbors the Ingush, Chechens belong to the Sunni sect of Islam. Russian empress Catherine the Great set out in 1783 to conquer the Caucasus. Chechens and other peoples of the region fought the Russians sporadically for nearly eighty years until they were finally defeated in 1859. The region became part of the Russian empire, although local people continued to rebel against their rulers.

Communists came to power in Russia in 1917 and later established the Soviet Union. In 1924, the Communists forced the Chechens and the Ingush to join the Soviet Union as the Chechen-Ingush Autonomous Republic. The Chechens and other Caucasus peoples hated the Soviets so much that many of them cooperated with German Nazi forces that invaded the area during World War II (1939–1945).

When the war ended, Soviet leader Josef Stalin punished six ethnic groups from the Caucasus—the Chechens, Ingush, Kalmyks, Karachays, Tatars, and Meskhetian Turks—for helping the

An Interview With A Terrorist Leader

In July 2005, the U.S. TV show *Nightline* ran an interview with Shamil Basayev, the Chechen Islamist terrorist who masterminded the Beslan school siege. In a conversation with Russian journalist Andrei Babitsky, the Chechen leader admitted, "I'm a bad guy, a bandit, a terrorist."

Basayev was born January 14, 1965, in Vedeno, in southeastern Chechnya, to a family that has opposed Russian rule for several generations. He has been a leader in fighting the Russians since the first Chechen War in 1994. In 2000, Besayev lost his right leg below the knee when he stepped on a landmine while withdrawing his men from a battle in Grozny, the capital of Chechnya. In the interview, he claimed that his tactics were the same as those the Russians used against the Chechens. Basayev said, "I will pull no punches to stop this genocide."

The interviewer asked Basayev if his campaign was mainly motivated by religion. Basayev said: "For me, it's first and foremost a struggle for freedom. If I'm not a free man, I can't live in my faith. I need to be a free man. Freedom is primary. That's how I see it. Sharia (Islamic law) comes second."

Nazis. He deported them to remote work camps in Central Asia and Siberia. As many as 800,000 Chechens were deported to work camps, where as many as 100,000 died from brutal living conditions. More than a million Caucasus Muslims were sent into exile in all. The survivors were allowed to return home in 1957, after Stalin's death. The deportations left many of the Caucasus peoples suspicious of the Russians and also of some of their neighbors, such as the Ossetians. Their suspicions lasted beyond the breakup of the Soviet Union in 1991.

Among the Chechens Stalin sent into exile was the family of Shamil Basayev. Basayev leads Riyad al-Salikhin, the group that carried out the Beslan school siege. In a July 2005 interview, Basayev said one reason he was fighting Russia was to prevent similar injustices. Making a reference to the Muslims who were exiled by Stalin, he said: "I need guarantees that tomorrow future Chechen generations won't be deported to [their deaths] like they were. That's why we need independence."

The First Chechen War

In 1991, when the Soviet Union broke up, Chechnya and other republics were claimed by the Russian Federation. Russia sees the republics in the Caucasus as a key safeguard to its southern border. The region, and the nearby Caspian Sea, is also an important source of oil and natural gas for Russia.

The Chechens, however, declared their independence. They formed the Chechen Republic of Ichkeria ("Ichkeria" is the Turkic name for the central part of the republic), in a mountainous region of about 5,000 square miles (13,000 square kilometers). They formed their own government and elected Dzhokhar Dudayev president.

Boris Yeltsin, president of the newly formed Russian Federation, rejected the declaration of independence. When Chechens continued to resist Yeltsin's

▲ Shamil Basayev is the leader of the Chechen separatist terrorist group that carried out the Beslan school siege.

demands to join the Russian Federation, Russia invaded Chechnya in 1994 with 40,000 soldiers. The Chechens fought back, beginning the first Chechen war. The conflict became expensive for Russia and unpopular with its citizens. In 1996, Russia withdrew its forces, although it did not grant Chechnya independence. The conflict cost the lives of about

80,000 Chechen soldiers and civilians and about 3,826 Russian soldiers.

The Chechens again declared the independence of the Chechen Republic of Ichkeria. In January 1997, they elected as president Aslan Maskhadov, a Chechen military commander who had played a key role in the war. Shamil Basayev, who was also a war leader, finished second in the voting. Maskhadov named Basayev prime minister, the second highest ranking post in the new government.

Splits Among the Chechens

Although Maskhadov and Basayev had both fought for independence, they had different ideas about the shape of the new nation. Their disagreements weakened the new government and prevented Chechens from uniting against Russia.

Maskhadov's government faced opposition from militant Islamists who wanted Chechnya to be governed by Sharia, the law of Islam. Maskhadov wanted Chechnya to be a secular nation run by constitutional laws. Basayev, who was a leading Islamist, resigned as prime minister after only six months and began creating a network of private military units that could help him win control of Chechnya. Basayev's men fought groups of government supporters, kidnapped their rivals, and tried to

Basayev, who was a leading Islamist, began creating a network of private military units

assassinate Maskhadov. In August 1999, Basayev and Ibn-ul Khattab, a Chechen raised in Jordan, led a small army into neighboring Dagestan to try to force it to join Chechnya in a new, larger Muslim nation.

Justification for a New War

On September 9, 1999, a series of apartment bombings in two Russian cities killed 293 people. President Vladimir Putin claimed that Chechen terrorists were responsible for the bombings and said he would punish the terrorists. He promised, "We'll get them anywhere." The official investigation found that the bombings had been planned by Arab terrorists fighting with the Chechen terrorists.

There was, however, little hard evidence for this claim. A few days later, police caught men planting sacks of explosives in the basement of an apartment building in the Russian town of Ryazan. The men were members of the Russian Federal Security Service (FSB). The FSB said that the operation was a training exercise. Investigations by French journalists, supported by opponents of Putin such as the businessman Boris Berezovsky, claim that the FSB planted all of the bombs to give Putin a justification for invading Chechnya.

In September 1999, Russian forces moved into Chechnya, starting the

The Black Widows

Many women have participated in Chechen terrorist attacks, including two who were among the terrorists in the Beslan siege. Chechen female terrorists have been nicknamed the Black Widows, after the venomous spider, because many of them have lost their husbands in the conflict with Russia. Their primary motivation is revenge. One of the Beslan terrorists was 45-year-old Khaula Nazirov. Her husband had been tortured to death by the Russians and her 18-year-old son and 16-year-old daughter were killed when Russia's planes bombed a school in Chechnya. The Black-Widow suicide bombers who blew up two airplanes in 2004 also lost their husbands in the conflict. The first Black Widow was Hawa Barayeva, who in June 2000 killed 27 Russian soldiers in a suicide bomb attack.

In 2003, a Chechen widow who called herself Kowa told a journalist how she felt after her husband's death: "I have only one dream now, one mission—to blow myself up somewhere in Russia, ideally in Moscow. To take as many Russian lives as possible—this is the only way to stop the Russians from killing my people. Maybe this way they will get the message and leave us alone, once and for all."

▼ Investigators search the wreckage of a Russian airliner blown up by a Black-Widow suicide bomber on August 25, 2004. The bombing killed 46 people.

▲ Chechen fighters ride on a captured tank as they celebrate the withdrawal of Russian forces in 1996, ending the first Chechen war.

second Chechen war. They used heavy artillery and jet planes to bomb Chechnya into submission. By February 2000, Chechnya's capital, Grozny, and other cities had been nearly destroyed and thousands of Chechens had been killed. Russia swiftly conquered Chechnya. Putin installed Akhmad Kadyrov as president to govern the republic.

Chechens and Terrorism

Russia's military occupation forced Chechen separatists to flee to the remote mountains in southern Chechnya, where they set up a government in exile led by President Maskhadov. Maskhadov entered into an uneasy alliance with Basayev and the Islamist warlords. The Russians claimed in 2005 that there were about 1,500 Chechen rebels in hiding. Human rights groups, however, say that the Russians often underestimate figures to make the Chechen cause appear poorly supported. The real number of rebels may be higher; they are supported by many Chechens.

The Chechen separatists fought the Russians with guerrilla-style hit-and-run tactics that killed several thousand Russian soldiers. Basayev and other Islamist warlords, such as Doku Umarov, also turned to terrorism. Unlike Maskhadov, the Islamists believed dramatic, violent acts would make the world aware of the Chechens' fight for independence and frighten Russian citizens into demanding that Russia leave Chechnya.

In an interview in 2005, Basayev claimed that terrorism was a legitimate part of the Chechens' "struggle for our national independence." He claimed that in reality, "It's the Russkies [Russians] who are the terrorists." Although 186 children died in the Beslan school siege, Basayev claimed that Russian soldiers had killed more than 40,000 Chechen children in the last decade. He said they died in artillery and air strikes during the Chechen wars; in raids against suspected terrorists; and from substandard living conditions the conflict has caused, such as poor medical care. There is no independent verification of Basayev's figures, which Russia denies.

In 2005, Taus Djabrailov, the leader of Chechnya's parliament, claimed that a total of between 150,000 and 160,000 people have died in the Chechen conflict since the collapse of the Soviet Union in 1992. The total includes Russian troops, Chechen rebels and terrorists, and civilians who were killed during military actions or murdered by Russia for backing the terrorists.

Not all Chechen separatists, however, believed that terrorism is justified, including Maskhadov. He condemned the Beslan siege as an act by "madmen" driven insane by Russian brutality. He said that none of the rebels he commanded had anything to do with it. On a Chechen Web site, Maskhadov said that Basayev should stand trial for the siege. He went on, however, "With the current war continuing, it is practically impossible to bring to justice those responsible for the terrorist act."

When soldiers stormed the building, 166 hostages were killed and Basayev and other terrorists escaped

Hostage Taking

The Beslan siege was not the first time Chechen terrorists took Russians hostage. In June 1995, six months after Russia invaded Chechnya in the first Chechen war, gunmen led by Basayev herded 1,500 people into a hospital in Budenovsk. When soldiers stormed the building in what many analysts think was a botched rescue, 166 hostages were killed and Basayev and other terrorists escaped. Many hostages died in the crossfire between soldiers and terrorists. The terrorists later took about 300 people hostage in another hospital, this time in Kizlyar in

Dagestan. This siege ended largely without bloodshed, as did the simultaneous hijacking of a ferry in the Black Sea with more than 255 hostages aboard.

Before the Beslan school siege, the most dramatic hostage situation created by Chechen terrorists began on October 23, 2002. Forty-one terrorists took more than 800 people prisoner during the performance of a play in a Moscow theater. The terrorists, some wearing belts full of explosives, threatened to shoot or blow up the hostages unless Russia agreed to withdraw from Chechnya. In a videotaped statement, the terrorists claimed, "Every nation has the right to their fate. Russia has taken away this right from the Chechens and today we want to reclaim these rights, which God has given us."

The crisis ended on October 27, when Russia's FSB pumped fast-acting gas into the theater to make everyone unconscious. Soldiers then stormed the theater. Putin claimed the raid had saved hundreds of people. But because the gas killed 130 hostages, many nations criticized Russia for not trying to end the siege peacefully with negotiations. All the terrorists also died, either from the gas or from being shot. A British newspaper reported a Russian special-forces officer saying that terrorists had been shot at close range while they were unconscious.

In spite of appearing to be a failure for the terrorists, the Moscow theater attack accomplished their goal of making the world aware of the Chechens' continuing battle with Russia. The attack also marked the first time that Chechen terrorists identified themselves as Riyad al-Salikhin, the same group that later carried out the Beslan siege. The group wants independence from Russian and the creation of an Islamic state in Chechnya.

> ## The terrorists, some wearing belts full of explosives, threatened to shoot or blow up the hostages

Other Terrorist Attacks

Another tactic favored by Chechen terrorists is suicide bombing. In a 24-hour period in July 2000, Chechen terrorists staged suicide attacks against five Russian military bases, one of which killed 54 soldiers near the Chechen capital of Grozny. Most Chechen suicide bombers have been women, including two terrorists who killed 15 people on July 5, 2003, at an outdoor rock concert in Moscow.

On May 9, 2004, Chechen terrorists assassinated Chechen president Akhmad Kadyrov, who was loyal to Russia. Kadyrov was blown up by a bomb in Grozny during a parade to celebrate the Allied victory over Germany in World War II. The assassination was a blow to Russia's attempt to restore order in Chechnya.

The Russians declared that the

The Death of Two Young Actors

Two victims in the Moscow theater siege were thirteen-year-old Arseny Kurilenko and fourteen-year-old Kristina Kurbatova, the teenage stars of the play that was being performed when terrorists seized the theater.

In *Nord-Ost* (North-East), Arseny played Sanya and Kristina was Katya, two young people who fall in love. In the months in which they acted together, Arseny and Kristina became very close friends. They were buried near each other on October 30, after a funeral attended by hundreds of mourners. The two young actors were among the best known of the 130 people who died when police pumped a gas into the theater in the rescue effort. They were also among those who the public mourned the most because they had died so young.

One young actor who survived was eleven-year-old Gleb Bauer. He brought flowers to the funeral of his costars. Even though Bauer escaped when the terrorists first attacked, the experience frightened him badly. He said at the funeral that he had trouble sleeping and was afraid. "I've been crying a lot, I cry all the time. I can't go anywhere," he said.

▼ Emergency workers carry injured and dead hostages out of the Moscow theater that was seized by Chechen terrorists.

Are International Terrorists Involved?

It has long been known that individual Muslims from around the world have traveled to Chechnya to join the rebels, who they see as fighting for Islam. By 2005, up to 200 foreign fighters were helping the Chechens. One notable foreign fighter was Ibn al-Khattab, who was born in Saudi-Arabia. Al-Khattab fought with Muslim rebels against the Russian occupation of Afghanistan before joining the Chechens in 1995. He served as a military commander until Russian forces assassinated him in March 2002 with a poisoned letter.

After the Beslan siege, Russian president Vladimir Putin and the FSB also claimed that the Chechens were aided by al-Qaeda. Al-Qaeda is the Islamist group led by Osama bin Laden that committed the September 11, 2001, terrorist attacks on the United States. The FSB said that Abu Omar as-Seif, whom it claimed was an al-Qaeda representative, funded the Beslan school siege.

Chechen terrorist leader Shamil Basayev, however, denied links with al-Qaeda. Although al-Khattab had met bin Laden in Afghanistan, no hard evidence exists that al-Qaeda or other international terrorist groups have provided substantial aid to the Chechens. Western analysts believe that Putin has tried to establish a link between Chechens and international terrorists to gain international support for his military actions in Chechnya.

elections to replace Kadyrov would be limited to candidates who supported Russia. Chechen separatist terrorists staged a series of attacks to protest the elections. On August 21, five days before the election, more than 200 separatist gunmen entered Grozny. They bombed a police station and voting centers, killing 11 people. On August 24, ninety people died when two Russian passenger planes exploded almost simultaneously in midair. Their deaths were blamed on female Chechen suicide bombers who were onboard the planes. On August 31, another female suicide bomber killed nine people outside a Moscow subway.

A group calling itself the Islambouli Brigades claimed responsibility for the airliner and subway bombings. The group said that the attacks were "part of the wave of support and assistance to the Chechen Muslims." The climax to the deadly string of terrorist acts in the summer of 2004 was the Beslan school siege.

Basayev Takes Control

On March 8, 2005, members of the FSB surrounded a home in Tolstoy-Yurt, a village near Grozny where Maskhadov was hiding. Although the FSB said it wanted to capture the rebel president, Maskhadov was killed in the

operation. After his death, President Alu Alkhanov, the Russian-backed candidate who had been elected to succeed Kadyrov, said that Maskhadov "was a terrorist against his own people." He said that the armed struggle Maskhadov had led was the reason for Chechens' suffering because it had caused Russia's occupation. However, although Maskhadov had opposed Russia militarily, he had always condemned terrorism.

Maskhadov's death may have been a prelude to more Chechen terrorism in the future. It left the separatist fight more firmly in the hands of leaders who support terrorism. On August 26, 2005, Basayev was appointed first deputy prime minister of the renegade

▲ After the FSB killed Aslan Maskhadov, they blew up the house where he had been hiding, probably to punish the family that had sheltered him.

government. He claimed responsibility for an attack on the city of Nalchik, the capital of the Kabardino-Balkaria region of the Northern Caucasus, that took place on October 13, 2005. About 210 armed militants attacked various targets in the city, including the airport. By the time 2,000 Russian troops restored order, 12 civilians and 24 members of the security forces had died. About 90 of the attackers died, and 36 of them were captured. Basayev promised similar attacks on Russian targets in the future.

CHAPTER THREE

Separatist Terrorists

The Chechens' struggle against the Russian Federation is only one of many separatist terrorist campaigns that have occurred around the world and that are still occurring in countries from Turkey to the Philippines. Many separatist movements have turned to terrorism to try to achieve their ends, although almost all of them also have a political organization. These movements often have wide support, because they tend to express the wishes of an ethnic or religious group that sees itself as oppressed by a government. Not all supporters of separatism, however, also support terrorism; many believe that their goals should be achieved through negotiation. But separatists such as Shamil Basayev in Chechnya, believe that terrorism is one of the most powerful weapons they have to make governments meet their demands.

Some of the world's longest-running separatist terrorist campaigns have involved Northern Ireland; the Basque Country, in northwestern Spain; and the island of Sri Lanka, in the Indian Ocean.

Nations and Peoples

Separatism is closely bound up with the idea of the nation-state, or country. Since about the fifteenth century, peoples have been creating nations. A nation is usually based on shared characteristics, bringing together a population that speaks the same language or belongs to the same ethnic group. Nations, however, tend to have fixed borders, whereas peoples are far more flexible. Languages and cultures mix or move around. Through history, the borders of many nations have eventually come to contain large

▼ The Real IRA, a terrorist group trying to split Northern Ireland from Great Britain so that it can join the Irish Republic, bombed the town of Omagh on August 15, 1998, killing twenty-nine people.

minorities that live among the dominant majority of people. Long ago, for example, Ireland came under British control. Today, most of Ireland is independent, but Northern Ireland is still part of Great Britain. Most of its people are Protestants who are loyal to the British government. But it has a minority who are Catholic, many of whom want to join the rest of Ireland.

Self-Determination

One of the most important historical developments of the twentieth century was the breakup of various empires that had ruled vast regions of Asia, Africa, and Europe. The process began at the end of World War I (1914–1918), with the defeat of the Austro-Hungarian and Ottoman Empires. The Austro-Hungarian Empire had ruled large parts of Europe, while the Ottoman Empire had ruled parts of Europe and Asia.

After the war, a conference was held in Paris, France, to draw up peace treaties and decide what would happen to the regions that had been ruled by the empires. At the conference, U.S. president Woodrow Wilson insisted that

▲ Members of Algeria's National Liberation Front (FLN) lead away French soldiers after ambushing their vehicle. Both sides in Algeria's War of Independence not only attacked their military enemies, but also used terrorist tactics against civilians.

the treaties should be based on the principle of self-determination. This idea means that, as much as possible, peoples should govern themselves. Many nations came into being or were revived, such as Czechoslovakia; Poland; and the Kingdom of Serbs, Croats, and Slovenes, later called Yugoslavia. The difficulties of allowing everyone self-determination, however, were soon apparent. The new Czech nation, for example, contained not only Czechs but also many Germans, who would have preferred to be governed by Germany.

Despite such problems, self-determination was established as a guiding principle of international affairs. It motivated campaigns for independence in European colonies in Asia and Africa, particularly after World War II (1939–1945) changed the international balance of power. In some places, such as the Southeast Asian nation of Indonesia, nationalists launched violent campaigns against the colonial power and its armed forces. In most cases such campaigns were not strictly terrorism; their main purpose was not to spread fear among a population. One exception came in the French colony of Algeria, where

Terrorism and Algerian Independence

In 1954, the Algerian Front de Libération National (FLN) launched an armed revolt against the French who governed Algeria as a colony. People of European descent, known as "colons," made up 10 percent of Algeria's population. The majority of the population were Algerian Muslims. While the FLN attacked French army posts, its members also began terrorizing people it suspected of supporting the French. It cut off their lips or noses, or slit their throats.

In 1955, the FLN sparked an uprising in the town of Philippeville in which rioters killed 123 Europeans. The French reacted violently, killing Algerians. Those killings, in turn, brought more support for the FLN. In 1956, the FLN carried out bombings and assassinations in the capital, Algiers.

The French security forces used torture to gather intelligence from suspected FLN terrorists, and many of those who were tortured were then killed. The French campaign greatly reduced FLN activities.

At the end of the 1950s, it became clear that the new French president, Charles de Gaulle, did not want Algeria to remain a French colony. His opponents responded with a new terror campaign. In 1961 and 1962, the Secret Army Organization (OAS) bombed Islamic targets in Algiers and France, killing about 1,200 Muslims and French soldiers and civilians. The group also tried to kill De Gaulle himself.

De Gaulle pressed ahead with his plans. In 1962, a ceasefire was proclaimed and a timetable put in place for Algerian independence, which came later that year. Terrorism in Algeria, however, did not end. Algerian Islamic and nationalist groups used violent tactics against each other.

both Muslim Algerians and French colonists launched widespread acts of terror against the civilian population.

Almost everywhere, the creation of new states left ethnic or religious minorities being governed by a ruling majority different from themselves. The minorities began to call for self-determination, like other groups who had lived as minorities within nation-states for a long time.

By the end of the 20th century, separatist terrorists were still active in Turkey, where Kurdish separatists bombed a tourist bus in 2005, and in Kashmir, on the border between India and Pakistan. Islamic terrorists in Kashmir sought to get rid of Indian influence on the region. In China's northwestern Xinjiang region, meanwhile, Turkic separatists were trying to create an Islamic state called East Turkestan. China accuses four different groups of carrying out over 200 terrorist acts since 1990, including bombings and assassinations of people linked to the Chinese government. In the Philippines, groups such as Abu Sayyaf are trying to establish an Islamic state in the south of the country. Abu Sayyaf has kidnapped many foreigners, for whom it demands ransom payments. It has also launched attacks against Filipinos, such as the bombing of a ferry in October 2004 that killed more than one hundred people.

Separatism in Ireland

One infamous act of terrorism was the assassination on August 27, 1979, of Lord Louis Mountbatten, a cousin of England's Queen Elizabeth. Mountbatten and three others were killed when a bomb exploded on his yacht near Mullaghmore, a fishing village in the Republic of Ireland. The Irish Republican Army (IRA) released a statement in which it took credit for the deadly blast and explained why it killed the member of the British royal family. The IRA described the operation as "discriminate," meaning carefully targeted, in contrast to indiscriminate acts that kill people regardless of who they are: "This operation is one of the discriminate ways we can bring to the attention of the English people the continuing occupation of our country."

The "Troubles"

The killing of Mountbatten is one of hundreds of terrorist acts the IRA has committed since 1970 in its ongoing battle to force England to allow Northern Ireland to become part

▲ In October 1984, the IRA bombed a hotel in Brighton where senior members of the British government were staying. The bomb narrowly missed killing British prime minister Margaret Thatcher.

of a united country with the Republic of Ireland, which occupies most of the island of Ireland.

The ongoing conflict that the Irish call the "Troubles" began in 1969, after rioting and armed clashes between Catholics, who make up about 40 percent of the population, and the majority Protestant population became common in Northern Ireland. The religion-based violence was a response to protests by Irish Catholics who claimed that Northern Ireland's Protestants—backed by the government of Great Britain, which is a Protestant country were systematically discriminating against them in jobs, housing, education, and other areas of their lives.

The seeds of Irish Catholic discontent had actually been festering since England conquered Ireland in the sixteenth century. The Irish were Catholic, spoke Gaelic, and had their own culture. Over several centuries of rule, the English stripped Irish people of most of their land and gave it to English newcomers. Until the early twentieth century, the British government allowed only Protestants to govern the country. They denied Irish Catholics many basic rights, such as the rights to speak their language and, at times, practice their faith.

After several unsuccessful attempts to win their freedom, Irish political leaders on January 21, 1919, again declared Ireland's independence. This time the power of the new concept of self-determination and the strong, stubborn resistance of Irish fighters led England to agree to a compromise to end the conflict. The Anglo-Irish Treaty in 1920 created the Republic of Ireland, an independent nation. England, however, retained a smaller northern part of Ireland, now known as Northern Ireland, which remains part of Great Britain.

Many Irish Catholics in both new nations were angry that Ireland had been forcibly divided. In the decades that followed the political division, Irish Catholics in Northern Ireland also became enraged at the way the Protestant-dominated government treated them. When the Troubles began, the IRA and several other groups brought that anger to life through its deadly acts of terrorism against British security forces and against mainly Protestant civilians.

The IRA believed that terrorism was the only weapon it had to free Northern Ireland

Terrorism From Both Sides

The IRA believed that terrorism was the only weapon it had that would force Great Britain to allow Northern Ireland to be reunited with the Republic of Ireland. Many Irish people who supported the IRA's nationalist goals believed they could be achieved peacefully through diplomacy and negotiation, however. The IRA's campaign of violence included beatings, bombings, kidnappings, assassinations, and armed assaults. Some of its main targets have been police and British soldiers. Through 2005, the IRA was accused of killing nearly 1,800 people, including 1,200 soldiers, police officers, and members of Protestant paramilitary organizations. The IRA also murdered about 600 civilians, most of them in random bombings. The IRA detonated car bombs in city streets, stores, and other public places in Northern Ireland and Britain. The bombs killed anyone unlucky enough to be in the vicinity, including other Catholics. In Northern Ireland, July 21, 1972, will forever be known as "Bloody Friday" because, on that day, twenty-two IRA bombs killed nine people and injured 130. The IRA killed nearly 500 people in 1972, making it the conflict's deadliest year.

IRA terrorism was soon met by Protestant terrorism from groups such as the Ulster Volunteer Force (UVF), the Ulster Defence Association (UDF), Orange Volunteers, and the Red Hand Defenders. They launched terrorist attacks intended to terrify the Catholic population into not supporting the IRA or into moving out of loyalist areas. On May 17, 1974, the UVF carried out bombings in Dublin and Monaghan in the Republic of Ireland that killed thirty-three people, the greatest loss of life on any single day in the conflict. And, in 1993, UDA members firing machine guns killed eight Catholics in a Northern Ireland bar in Greysteel. Protestant terrorists killed more people in Northern Ireland each year in the 1990s than did the IRA.

The Basques

The Basques of northeastern Spain have also used terrorism to try to frighten their enemy into granting them a nation they can call their own. Like the IRA, the Euskadi Ta Askatasuna (in the Basque language, "Basque Fatherland and Liberty"), or ETA, has relied heavily on bombs to lend power to its attacks. One of its most infamous bombings came on December 20, 1973, when ETA killed Spanish prime minister Carrero Blanco by blowing up his car. ETA does not only attack political targets. Its deadliest attack occurred on June 19, 1987, when a bomb in the parking area of the Hipercor shopping mall in Barcelona killed 21 people and injured 45 more.

The bombings were part of a battle the Basques have waged since 1975, when Spanish dictator Francisco Franco died. The Basques had suffered greatly under Franco, who banned their language and imprisoned intellectuals

> **Protestant terrorists killed more people in Northern Ireland each year in the 1990s than did the IRA**

and political leaders who fought to preserve Basque culture. Euskera, the Basque language, is not related to other European languages, and Basque customs differ markedly from those of Spain and France, the two nations in which the Basque homeland lies.

ETA was founded in the late 1950s, and began carrying out assassinations in the 1960s. The Basques were treated better when democracy came to Spain after Franco's death. ETA then split. Some of its members abandoned terrorism and embraced democracy. In return, Spain's government pardoned some ETA supporters supsected of terrorist acts. ETA's military wing, however, became even more violent in its dedication to forcing Spain to grant Basque independence. Its members believed the Basques needed their own country so their heritage would never be so endangered again as it had been under Franco. To accomplish this, they waged a bloody campaign to create a new nation out of seven regions in northern Spain and southwest France

▼ Spanish police examine the wreckage of a car blown up by ETA in Madrid in August 2000. The bomb, which injured eleven people, was one of three ETA devices that exploded within 24 hours.

that are currently inhabited by 2.1 million Basques.

Since 1972, it is estimated that ETA terrorists have killed 848 people. There was hope the violence would end in September 1998, when ETA leaders declared a ceasefire in hopes of negotiating with Spain to establish a Basque nation. Jose Maria Robbes, a Spanish political leader, greeted the announcement with skepticism, claiming, "We don't trust them and we don't believe their word."

When negotiations with Spain's government faltered, ETA returned to terrorism in November 1999. Although ETA has killed 46 people since then, its level of violence has declined dramatically from the late 1970s, when the group killed 100 people a year. There have been no ETA terrorist deaths since 2003, when the group was responsible for killing three people. ETA, however, was still perpetrating minor acts of violence, such as detonating two bombs in Madrid in July 2005 to disrupt traffic.

Spain's government reported in 2004 that ETA terrorism had cost Spain's economy over $9 billion, largely through disrupting business, over the previous decade. More than one third of that total came from abandoning a project to build a nuclear power plant after ETA kidnapped and killed one of the project's engineers in 1981.

ETA remains highly dangerous, however, and still casts fear over Spain's society. When bombs blew up four commuter trains in Madrid, Spain's capital, on March 11, 2004, killing 191 people and injuring 1,800 more, the

▼ A car burns after an ETA attack in Madrid, Spain, in 1993. Car bombs are one of ETA's favored means of killing its targets.

country's government blamed ETA for the blast. ETA denied involvement, and it was later discovered that the bombers were Moroccan Islamists who were tied to al-Qaeda.

The Tamil Tigers

Halfway across the world from Europe is the island of Sri Lanka, which lies off the coast of India. Since 1985, it has been wracked by terrorism at the hands of the Liberation Tigers of Tamil Eelam (LTTE). The Tamils are a

minority ethnic group who seek their own nation; "Eelam" means homeland in the Tamil language. About one-fifth of Sri Lanka's population is Tamil. Their religion Hinduism and language differ from those of the majority Sinhalese, who are mainly Buddhist and speak Sinhala.

In addition to fielding a guerrilla army that helps them control part of Sri Lanka, the Tamil Tigers engage in terrorist attacks. They have depended heavily on suicide bombings, carrying

Separatism in Quebec

In the 1960s and 1970s, separatist terrorism came to North America when the Quebec Liberation Front (FLQ) carried out a series of bombings, kidnappings, and murders. The FLQ wanted Quebec, which has a French-speaking majority, to become independent of the rest of Canada, where the majority of people speak English. The FLQ used terrorism to try to scare away the English-Canadian businesses that dominated the Quebecois economy.

In 1963, the FLQ began a bombing campaign that blew up mailboxes and public buildings in Montreal, the largest city in Quebec. One bomb at an army recruiting center killed a security guard. Partly as a result of public debate begun by the FLQ, the movement for Quebec separatism gained political momentum. The provincial government took control of key industries on behalf of the French-speaking majority in the mid-1960s.

The FLQ, meanwhile, became more ambitious. It sent members to train with Palestinian terrorists in the Middle East. In 1968, the FLQ began another bombing campaign, which included a blast at the Montreal stock exchange that injured nearly 30 people.

The peak of FLQ's terrorist activity came in October 1970. It kidnapped James Cross, Britain's trade commissioner in Canada, and Pierre Laporte, the labor minister in Quebec's provincial government. The FLQ demanded a large ransom and release of FLQ prisoners. When its demands were not met, it murdered Laporte. Cross was released two months later after the Canadian and Quebecois governments launched a concerted campaign against the FLQ. The group's activities largely ceased following the kidnappings.

Do Separatists Deserve Sympathy?

Although people around the world generally hate terrorists because they kill innocent people, separatist terrorists often win some sympathy because the governments of the countries in which they live deny their rights or treat them harshly. Some countries have been less critical toward Chechen terrorists because of the wars Russia has waged in Chechnya.

On January 10, 2002, U.S. State Department spokesman Richard Boucher talked about reports from Chechnya of Russia's "continuation of human rights violations and the use of overwhelming force against civilian targets." He said that "massive human rights violations [by Russians], we believe, contribute to an environment that is favorable toward terrorism."

Boucher was not supporting terrorism, but he may have been pointing out that people sometimes turn to terrorism because they feel they have no other way to fight back against a powerful opponent. Russia, however, argues that the Chechen terrorists are no different from other terrorists that kill civilians indiscriminately. President Vladimir Putin called them "child killers."

In 2004, British journalists asked Putin why he did not negotiate with Chechen separatists. He answered by contrasting the suggestion with the West's military response to the attacks launched by Osama bin Laden's al-Qaeda organization in the United States on September 11, 2001. Putin said he thought the West had double standards in expecting him to talk to terrorists. He asked, "Why don't you meet Osama bin Laden, invite him to Brussels or to the White House and engage in talks, ask him what he wants and give it to him so he leaves you in peace?"

out about 200 such attacks in two decades. Tamil–Tiger attacks have occurred at Buddhist shrines and office buildings, including a 1997 suicide truck bomb that killed eighteen people at the World Trade Center in Colombo, Sri Lanka's capital.

The Tigers have also assassinated many political leaders who opposed them, including former prime minister of India Rajiv Gandhi. Gandhi was killed in May 1991 by a suicide bomber after he sent India's army to Sri Lanka to act as peacekeepers. Another high-profile Tiger victim was Sri Lanka's president, Ranasinghe Premadasa, who was killed by a suicide bomber in May 1993. The Tigers are also suspected in the shooting death on August 12, 2005, of Lakshman Kadirgamar, Sri Lanka's foreign minister. Kadirgamar was a Tamil who opposed terrorism and worked with Sri Lanka's government to help improve life for Tamils. Although the Tigers denied killing him, most

observers believe the group commit the murder. They had tried to murder him several times before for his outspoken opposition to their activities. Kadirgamar had been influential in persuading the U.S. and British governments to outlaw the Tigers as a terrorist group.

Reaction to Terrorism

Separatist terrorists who commit violent acts like the assassination of Kadirgamar justify them by claiming they are a necessary part of their wars for independence. Most people around the world, however, view these acts very differently. U.S. Secretary of State Condoleezza Rice reacted strongly to Kadirgarmar's death, calling it a "senseless murder and vicious act of terror." Rice also praised Kadirgamar, whom she had met in June in Washington, D. C., when they talked

▲ Members of the Tamil Tigers in training. The group sees itself as a military force, although it also carries out terrorist attacks.

about relief aid for Sri Lankan victims of the 2004 tsunami. "He was a man of dignity, honor and integrity, who devoted his life to bringing peace to Sri Lanka," said Rice.

Rice's attitude reflected the official U.S. stance against all terrorism. Most people who are not government leaders also consider acts of terrorism to be senseless and brutal. Leontia Hay is a nurse in Northern Ireland who has treated victims of IRA bombs. After one incident, Hoy asked the question most people ponder after a terrorist attack: "Please tell me what this bombing achieved other than sorrow, nightmares, and hardship to all involved?"

CHAPTER FOUR

Responses to Separatist Terrorism

On the first anniversary of the final day of the Beslan school siege Russian President Vladimir Putin made a startling admission about his country's inability to prevent such devastating acts of terrorism. "I agree with those who believe that the state is not in a condition to provide for the security of its citizens to the necessary degree," said Putin. He made the comment in Moscow on September 3, 2005, before meeting with three members of the Committee of Beslan Mothers, all of whom had children who died in the siege. The group of 150 mothers blames Putin and other officials for mistakes that allowed the siege to happen and result in more deaths than were necessary.

That day, Putin also made a startling claim about the vulnerability of the entire world to terrorism. Putin said that even the most advanced, richest, and most powerful nations "cannot prevent terrorist attacks today." As proof, Putin pointed to the September 11, 2001, terrorist attacks in the United States that killed nearly 3,000 people; the March 11, 2004, bombings in Madrid, Spain, that claimed the lives of 191 people; and the July 7, 2005, bombings in London, England, in which over 50 people died.

A Failure by Russia?

Many people believed that Putin was trying to avoid blame for mishandling the Beslan siege. On the first anniversary of the terror attack, charges of Russian incompetence and questions about what really

▼ Mourners light candles at a memorial service for the victims of the Beslan school siege.

happened overshadowed the numbing grief that the people of Beslan still felt for the hostages who were killed.

One of the fiercest critics of the Russian handling of the siege has been Stanislav Kesaev, a North Ossetian official who chaired an investigation into the crisis. Kesaev claimed that security forces bungled the end of the siege. "The coordination between the different arms of the security forces was absolutely awful," he charged.

The majority of hostages who died in the disaster were killed in the deadly crossfire between terrorists and soldiers, police, and armed Beslan residents who stormed the school. Kesaev and others said that the operation was so poorly planned that the security forces unnecessarily killed many hostages. Andrey Kokoev, a police officer in North Ossetia's Organized Crime Department who was sent to Beslan, said he and other officers received no guidance in the battle. "It was all spontaneous. We had no orders," he said.

Kesaev and others have also claimed the Russian authorities made the hostage situation worse by refusing to

negotiate in good faith with the terrorists and caring more about killing terrorists to end the siege than saving lives. One of the negotiators, former president of Ingushetia Ruslan Aushev, accused Russia of wasting time before they spoke to the terrorists. If the security forces had discovered the terrorists' demands earlier, he said, "We would have had time for more ideas."

Why Did the Shooting Start?

The events that sparked the storming of the school by Russian forces are still controversial. The official account from Russia's forces claims that a bomb in

the gymnasium accidentally exploded. Accounts by some hostages and witnesses, however, claim that a sniper shot a terrorist through a school window and the wounded terrorist's foot then slipped off a safety device that had kept a bomb from exploding.

When the bomb went off, the storming began and many hostages died needlessly. Ruslan Aushev said that he believed that armed civilians started the shooting after the first explosion. He said, "The official forces were not shooting, the captors were not shooting, and we were yelling at each other, 'Who's doing the shooting?'"

One year after the siege, the cause of the pivotal first explosion was just one of many key facts in the official version of what happened that was being disputed. Some hostages and other witnesses claimed there were at least 50 attackers, not 32, and that some of them escaped on the final day. These accounts also alleged that terrorists used weapons that had been hidden in the school by accomplices.

Questions remained even though there had already been several investigations into what happened. When Putin met with Beslan mothers in Moscow, he promised he would authorize another probe to find out

◀ Russian security forces, members of which are seen here in position during the Beslan siege, were heavily criticized for the high number of casualties during the operation to end the crisis.

what happened. "He assured us that the truth will be uncovered," said Susana Dudiyeva, one of the mothers who met with him. Her thirteen-year-old son, Zaurbek, died in the siege.

Protection Against Attack

Although it is rare for Russian officials to admit they have made a mistake, Putin's remarks on the anniversary of the Beslan siege were not his first admission of failure in Russia's anti-terrorism effort. Just a few days after the siege ended, Putin declared, "We have achieved practically no visible results in our fight against terror." In the next few months, Putin acted to strengthen Russia's anti-terror campaign.

Putin sent more soldiers to Chechnya, tightened security measures to make it harder for terrorists to move around Russia, and devised a system of security alerts to warn people about terrorism threats. Putin also stepped up efforts to capture Chechen terrorists. In addition, Russia also increased the reward for the capture of Shamil Basayev, who planned the Beslan siege, to $10 million.

Tightening security to make it harder for terrorists to travel to their targets, as Russia did, is an important way in which many nations fight separatist terrorists. Another important tactic is called "target-hardening,"

Putin declared, "We have achieved practically no visible results in our fight against terror"

which makes it more difficult for terrorists to attack targets such as airports and other mass transit facilities, government offices, and public places such as stores, restaurants, and schools. Potential targets can be protected with concrete barriers that keep car bombs at a safe distance; high-tech machines that detect bombs or other weapons; bomb-sniffing dogs; and government or private security guards. In London, for example, the Irish Republican Army (IRA) used bombs hidden in cars and trucks to blow up financial buildings in the early 1990s. The police responded by setting up a security cordon around the financial district, with road blocks at which officers can check vehicles driving into the area.

Controversial Measures

Terrorists such as the IRA and the Basque group Euskadi Ta Askatasuna (ETA) live within the countries they set out to attack, so those countries can introduce specific laws or policies to try to deal with them. Sometimes, however, such measures may be unfair or abusive. In 1971, for example, the British government introduced a policy called internment in Northern Ireland. This policy allowed security forces to detain suspected terrorists without trial. It was used mainly against Catholics; nearly 2000

▲ Six million Spaniards, including these people, took to the streets to protest ETA's killing of Basque politicians in July 1997.

many of which ended in violence. The Irish government and international courts condemned internment as an abuse of human rights. Other countries have faced similar criticism for the way in which they tackled separatist terrorists. In the early 1970s, for example, the Canadian government was criticized for using wartime measures in its fight against separatists in Quebec. The measures suspended many principles of normal justice.

The British also tried to defeat Irish terrorism by militarizing Northern Ireland. Army units patrolled the streets of Belfast and other cities. The IRA called the action an "occupation," and it caused much resentment and might have encouraged the terrorism it was intended to halt.

British security forces had more success with infiltrating both Catholic and Protestant terror groups. Using informants, they gathered intelligence that helped them discover places where weapons were hidden and disrupt planned operations.

Public Pressure

Around the world, separatist groups who turn to terrorism often draw criticism from people who support their goals but reject the use of violence. In 1997, in Spain, for example, ETA killed a young Basque politician opposed to separatism and kidnapped and killed another. The killings triggered a series of huge public demonstrations. About 25,000 Basques, many of whom were likely

Catholics were locked up, compared to only 100 Protestants. The policy, which was in place until 1975, caused demonstrations among Catholic communities in Northern Ireland,

A New Attitude Toward Separatist Terrorists?

Terrorism experts believe that one factor that has pushed some separatist terrorists to join a peace process is a new attitude toward terrorism among the general public. Michael Swetnam of the Potomac Institute of Policy Studies in Arlington, Virginia, said in July 2005 that he believes dramatic terrorist attacks in the United States, Spain, and England have given people everywhere a far more negative image of all terrorists.

Swetnam said separatist terrorists were once seen almost sympathetically as freedom fighters using violence against a government that was abusing them. He said people now see separatist terrorists as no different from any other terrorists.

Swetnam believes the public backlash has begun to make separatist groups who previously used terror tactics to abandon them. Magnus Ranstorp, a terrorism expert who teaches at St. Andrews in Scotland, agreed. He said that separatists realized that the depth of feeling against terrorism had deepened so much that their supporters might turn against them if they staged an attack that killed many innocent people.

sympathetic to the idea of Basque independence, marched to show their rejection of terrorism. Outside the Basque region, a total of about six million people marched in the streets of Spain's cities to protest ETA's terrorist campaign.

Under public pressure, and also influenced by the peace process then underway in Northern Ireland, ETA's leadership called a ceasefire. The group held talks with Spanish political parties. When the government did not become involved in the talks, however, ETA resumed its campaign of violence. In 2001, it assassinated two senior national politicians, and, in 2003, it launched a series of bombings of targets related to Spain's valuable tourist industry.

Spain's security forces meanwhile cooperated with their French counterparts to combat ETA. A joint operation led to the arrest in October 2004 of sixteen members of ETA. Spanish Interior Minister Jose Antonio Alonso credited the way the two countries worked together for making the operation a success. "The arrests are part of an excellent collaboration between Spain and France in anti-terrorism policies," he said.

Hopes for Peace in 2005

One way to reduce separatist violence is by negotiating with the terrorists. Most governments have a public policy of not dealing with terrorists, but many have held secret talks with separatist terrorists. Separatist terrorists

Terrorism and Peace Efforts

When the Irish Republican Army (IRA) on July 28, 2005, declared it would end terrorism, British prime minister Tony Blair said he hoped "this may be the day when . . . peace replaces war, politics replaces terror [in] Ireland." The Irish were already aware, however, how fragile peace can be. The same hopes were raised on April 10, 1998, when the IRA agreed to a ceasefire to negotiate with Britain. But, on August 15, 1998, a breakaway terrorist band called the Real IRA killed twenty-nine people in a bomb blast in Omagh.

The Omagh bombing led Martin McGuinness, a Sinn Fein spokesman who had previously been a senior member of the IRA, to issue the republican movement's strongest condemnation ever of terrorism. "This appalling act," McGuinness said, "was carried out by those opposed to the peace process." The Real IRA had split from the IRA itself because it disapproved of the peace process. It still believed the best way to win union with Ireland was to continue a campaign of terrorism.

have sometimes proved willing to abandon violence in return for concessions that stop short of independence. Britain's government began secret meetings with the IRA as long ago as 1972. During the 1990s, the meetings became more frequent and more open. Britain set up the Northern Ireland Assembly to give Catholics more of a say in governing the region. After negotiations, the IRA called a ceasefire in 1994. It resumed terrorism in London, Manchester, and Northern Ireland in 1996 after further talks failed to make progress. A new ceasefire followed in 1997, and the political wing of the IRA, Sinn Fein, met the British prime minister for the first official talks.

Although Sinn Fein has joined the Northern Irish Assembly, the Protestant community remains suspicious of the possibility of further IRA terrorism. On July 28, 2005, the IRA pledged to end its terrorist campaign. Claiming, "We are conscious that many people suffered in this conflict," the IRA said it would put down its guns and bombs and work "to build a just and lasting peace."

Britain's government responded by saying that it would withdraw 10,000 British soldiers from Northern Ireland. Irish Catholics resent the troops because of episodes such as "Bloody Sunday," in 1972, during which soldiers killed thirteen Catholics while trying to restore order during a protest against internment.

Northern Ireland is not the only country that can hope for an end to separatist terrorist violence. In June 2005, ETA announced a partial ceasefire in which it said it would no

longer try to kill politicians who opposed its goals. It did that so negotiations could begin with the Spanish government to bring the conflict to a peaceful conclusion.

In Sri Lanka, a ceasefire that began in February 2002 continued in 2005 despite the assassination by the Tamil Tigers of Foreign Minister Laksham Kadirgamar on August 12, 2005. One reason the ceasefire has held is that everyone in Sri Lanka has been forced to work together to help the nation recover from the devastating December 2004 tsunami. The tsunami damaged Tamil areas badly, and the government sent aid to the region. Although the

▲ Gerry Adams, president of Sinn Fein, after voting in 2003 elections for the Northern Ireland Assembly. Adams's party, which was formerly the political wing of the IRA, said it was committed to democratic politics.

ceasefire continued, peace talks broke down after Kadirgamar's assassination. Douglas Devananda, the only Tamil official left in Sri Lanka's government, was not hopeful about the peace process. Devananda, who has survived ten assassination attempts by the Tamil Tigers, said that there was only one sure method to stop terrorism: "The [rebels] should be just annihilated. There is no other way."

Time Line

1991	December: Breakup of the former Soviet Union.
1992	Chechens declare independent Chechen Republic of Ichkeria.
1994	Russian troops invade Chechnya, beginning first war.
1995	June: Chechen terrorists take 1,500 people hostage in a hospital in Budenovsk.
1996	Russia withdraws its forces from Chechnya.
1997	January: Aslan Maskhadov elected as Chechen president.
1999	September: Bombs kill 293 people in Russian cities. Russia invades Chechnya in response.
2000	Russian forces conquer Chechnya and install Akhmad Kadyrov as president. June: First Chechen Black Widow becomes a suicide bomber.
2002	October 23: Chechen terrorists take more than 800 people hostage in a Moscow theater. October 27: Moscow theater siege ends when Russian troops storm the building; 130 hostages die in the rescue operation.
2004	May 9: Chechen terrorists assassinate president Akhmad Kadyrov. August 24: Chechen suicide bombers simultaneously destroy two Russian airliners in midair. September 1: Chechen terrorists seize about 1,100 people in a school in Beslan, North Ossetia, Russia. September 3: Russian special forces storm the school; about 330 people die in the gunfire and explosions.
2005	March 8: Russian intelligence forces kill Aslan Maskhadov. July: Nightline runs a controversial interview with Chechen terrorist leader Shamil Basayev. August 26: Shamil Basayev becomes Chechen deputy president. October 13: Separatist terrorists attack targets in Nalchik, capital of Kabardino-Balkaria.

Glossary

colonial: related to the areas controlled an empire governed by a dominant power.

communism: an economic system based on shared ownership and regulation by the state.

deport: to legally send someone out of a country.

diplomacy: peaceful political negotiations between countries.

government in exile: a government set up outside a territory that it claims the right to run but that actually has a different government.

guerrilla war: a war fought by unconventional means, such as ambushes and small-scale attacks on scattered targets.

hostage: a person who is held against his or her will to ensure that the hostage-taker's demands are met.

human rights: basic rights to which everyone is entitled, such as freedom from torture or unfair imprisonment.

independence: the ability, right, or sovereignty of a nation-state to govern its own affairs.

internment: confinement that resembles imprisonment, but without a trial or legal sentence.

Islamist: a Muslim who believes that Islam should be the basis of all forms of government and culture.

Muslim: a follower of Islam.

occupation: the control of one country by the military forces of another.

renegade: rejecting lawful behavior or authority.

republic: in the Russian Federation, one of the 21 areas in the country that has some power to govern itself but which is also subject to the federal government in Moscow.

self-determination: the right of a people or ethnic group to govern itself.

sharia: the legal system based on Islamic teachings.

tsunami: a tidal wave created by an earthquake beneath the sea.

Further Reading

Books

Anderson, Wayne. *The ETA: Spain's Basque Terrorists* (Inside the World's Most Famous Terrorist Organizations). Rosen Publishing Group, 2002.

Cottrell, Robert C., et al. *Northern Ireland and England: The Troubles* (Arbitrary Borders: Political Boundaries in World History). Chelsea House Publications, 2004.

Derkins, Susie. *The Irish Republican Army* (Inside the World's Most Infamous Terrorist Organizations). Rosen Publishing Group, 2002.

Hewitt, Christopher, and Tom Cheetham. *Encyclopedia of Modern Separatist Movements*. ABC-Clio Inc, 2000.

Nekov, Vesselin, and Paul Wilson. *57 Hours: A Survivor's Account of the Moscow Hostage Drama*. Penguin Putnam, 2004.

Web Sites

Times **Online Special Report: Beslan: The Aftermath**
www.timesonline.co.uk/article/
0,,2099-1385297,00.html

Tragedy at Beslan–September 1, 2004
www.beslan.ru/index.php?lang_id=1
&PHPSESSID=2778ae56f2f2404560
a6f0bda8ac90bf

CBS News: Beslan School Terror
www.cbsnews.com/stories/2005/01/
20/48hours/main668127.shtml

Guardian **Unlimited: Beslan School Tragedy**
www.guardian.co.uk/russia/beslan

BBC News: Beslan School Siege
news.bbc.co.uk/1/shared/spl/hi/
world/04/russian_s/html/1.stm

PBS Online NewsHour: Conflict in Chechnya
www.pbs.org/newshour/bb/europe/
chechnya/index.html

PBS Wide Angle: Greetings from Grozny
www.pbs.org/wnet/wideangle/
shows/chechnya/index.html

Index

Page numbers in *italics* refer to captions.

Abu Sayyaf 28
Adams, Gerry *43*
Algeria *26*–27
Alkhanov, Alu 23
al-Qaeda 22
Anglo-Irish Treaty (1920) 29
Aushev, Ruslan 9, 38
Austro-Hungarian Empire 25

Barayeva, Hawa 17
Basayev, Shamil 14, *15*, 16, 19, 22,
    23, 39
Basques 30–33, 40–41
Bauer, Gleb 21
Berezovsky, Boris 16
Beslan school siege *4*–11, 12, *36*–39
    eyewitness accounts 8
    leader of 14, *15*
Black Widows *17*
Blanco, Carrero 30
Bloody Friday 30
Bloody Sunday 42
Brighton bombing *28*
Budenovsk, siege in 19

Chechen separatist terrorists *4*, 5,
    18–23
    women *17*
    see also Beslan school siege

Chechen war
    first 14–16, *18*, 19
    second 18
Chechnya
    history 5–6, 12–18
    Muslims 5
China 27–28
colonies, independence 26
Cross, James 33
Czechoslovakia 26

Dagestan 16
Devananda, Douglas 43
Djabrailov, Taus 19
Dudayev, Dzhokhar 15

ETA 30, *31*, *32*–33, *40*, 41, 42–43

FLN (National Liberation Front), of
    Algeria *26*, 27
Franco, Francisco 30–31
FSB (Russian Federal Security Service)
    16, 20

Gandhi, Rajiv 34
Gaulle, Charles de 27
Grozny *12*, 18, 22

Hoy, Leontia 35

Ichkeria, Chechen Republic of 15, 16
Indonesia 26

IRA *see* Irish Republican Army
Ireland, Northern *24*, 25, 28–30, 40
    internment 39–40
Ireland, Republic of 29
Irish Republican Army (IRA) *28*–30,
    39, 40, 42, *43*
Islambouli Brigades 22

Kadirgamar, Lakshman 34–35
Kadyrov, Akhmad 18, 20–22
Kashmir 27
Kesaev, Stanislav 37–38
Khattab, Ibn al- 22
Kizlyar, siege in 19–20
Kulayev, Nur-Pashi 11
Kurbatova, Kristina 21
Kurilenko, Arseny 21

Laporte, Pierre 33

Maskhadov, Aslan 16, 18, 19
    death 22–23
Moscow theater siege 20, *21*
Muslims, Chechen 5

Nalchik 23
Nazirov, Khaula 17

Omagh bombing *24*, 42
Ossetians 14
Ottoman Empire 25

Philippeville 27
Philippines 28
Poland 26
Premadasa, Ranasinghe 34
Putin, Vladimir 16
    and the Beslan school siege 6–7, 9,
        12, 22, 36–37, 38–39
    and the Moscow theater siege 20

Quebec, separatism 33, 40

Real IRA *24*, 42
Rice, Condoleezza 35
Riyad al-Salikhin 5, 14, 20
Roshal, Leonid 9
Russian Federal Security Service (FSB)
    16, 20
Russian Federation
    and Chechnya 5–6, 14, 15–19
    see also Putin, Vladimir

separatist terrorists 24–35
    Chechen *4*, 5, *17*, 18–23
    responses to 36–43
Spain, Basque separatists *see* ETA
Sri Lanka, Tamil Tigers 33–*35*, 43
suicide bombers *17*, 20, 22
Swetnam, Michael 41

Tamil Tigers 33–*35*, 43
terrorists 4
    see also separatist terrorists
Turkey 27

Ulster Defence Association (UDA) 30
Ulster Volunteer Force (UVF) 30

Wilson, Woodrow 25–26

Yeltsin, Boris 15
Yugoslavia 26